The Great Glen Way

Jacquetta Megarry

Rucksack Readers

The Great Glen Way: Official Rucksack Reader Guide

First edition published 2001 by Rucksack Readers, Landrick Lodge, Dunblane, FK15 0HY, UK
Telephone   01786 824 696 (+44 1786 824 696)
Fax   01786 825 090 (+44 1786 825 090)
Email   info@rucsacs.com
Website   www.rucsacs.com

British Library cataloguing in publication data: a catalogue record for this book is available from the British Library.

ISBN 1-898481-07-5

Design by WorkHorse Productions (info@workhorse.co.uk)
Reprographics by Digital Imaging, printed by M&M Press Ltd, Glasgow on waterproof, biodegradable paper
The maps in this book were created for the purpose by Cartographic Consultants © 2001.

Publisher's note

This book was first published one year in advance of the Way's official opening. It describes the planned route as accurately as circumstances allowed at the time, and facts were checked carefully. However, things are bound to change, and readers' comments and suggestions are warmly invited. All contributions will be acknowledged in our second edition. Meanwhile, walkers are advised to check with the official website for updates and advice before setting out:

www.greatglenway.com

Anyone who walks on the Way before its official opening (Spring 2002) is reminded that it will not be waymarked and may not be complete. You are asked to respect the rights and convenience of land-owners. Even a few thoughtless walkers can threaten the co-operation and trust that has been built up over years.

The weather in Scotland is unpredictable year-round. Some parts of the Way may be wet underfoot, other parts are exposed and somewhat remote. You are responsible for your own safety, and for ensuring that your clothing, food and equipment are suited to your needs.

The Great Glen Way: contents

Long Distance Routes in Scotland

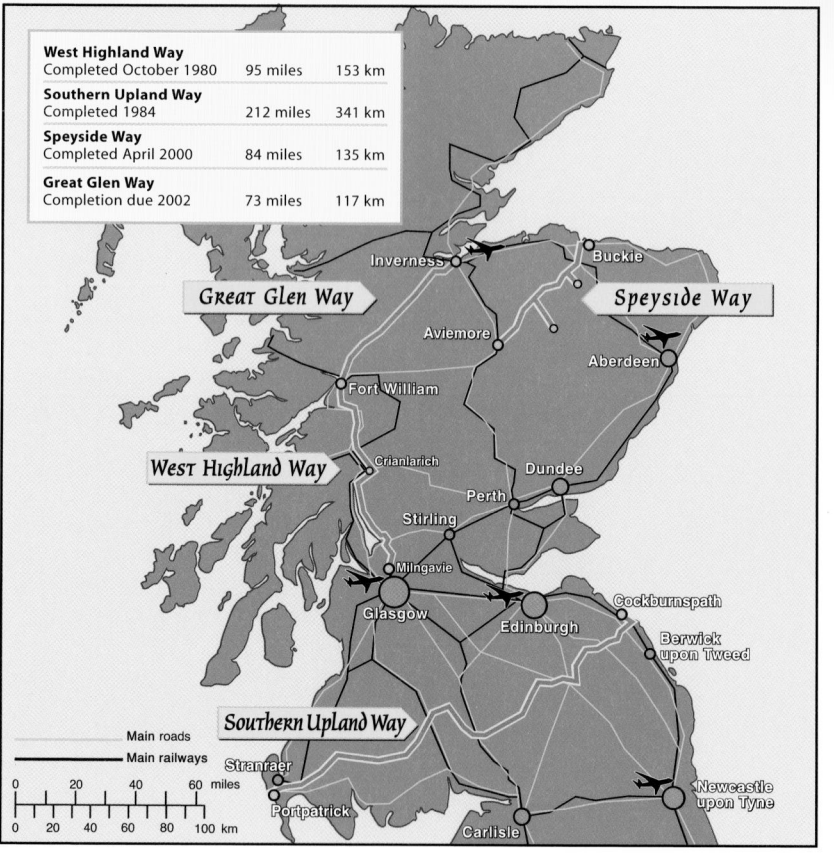

West Highland Way		
Completed October 1980	95 miles	153 km
Southern Upland Way		
Completed 1984	212 miles	341 km
Speyside Way		
Completed April 2000	84 miles	135 km
Great Glen Way		
Completion due 2002	73 miles	117 km

Long Distance Routes run like threads through Scotland's history. Walk one to follow in the footsteps of drovers, pilgrims, soldiers, clansmen and cattle-rustlers. The map shows Scotland's four official waymarked Long Distance Routes. The Great Glen Way runs 73 miles from Fort William to Inverness.

Funding for its creation came from the European Agricultural Guidance and Guarantee Fund under the Highlands and Islands Objective One Partnership Programme, Scottish Natural Heritage, Lochaber Ltd, and Inverness and Nairn Enterprise, with in-kind support from Forest Enterprise and British Waterways Board. The Great Glen Way is managed by Highland Council with grant assistance from Scottish Natural Heritage.

Planning to walk the Way

The Great Glen Way passes Britain's highest mountain, follows its greatest geological fault along the shores of its most famous loch and finishes at Inverness, Scotland's newest city and the capital of the highlands. Most of the walking is straightforward, along canal towpaths and forest tracks, but there are some challenging sections.

You don't need to be an experienced long-distance walker to tackle this hike. It is easier than the West Highland Way, for example, being shorter, flatter and mainly on good terrain. If you are not an experienced walker, read the 'Notes for novices' (pages 11-19). Well in advance of doing the Great Glen Way, you should complete a few long hikes, if only to test your feet and gear.

Experienced walkers may seize the chance to combine both Great Glen and West Highland Ways, walking from Glasgow to Inverness over two weeks (see page 63 for further reading and contacts). This challenging project takes you through 168 miles of spectacular scenery and highland heritage. It is arguably the grandest walk in Britain.

No-one should undertake the Great Glen Way casually, because the weather in Scotland is so unpredictable. On any given day in the highlands, you may experience weather typical of any season, and perhaps all four. This adds charm and variety to the experience, but also makes it important to have the right gear (page 14).

This book has been planned in the recommended direction, walking north-east from Fort William to Inverness. The prevailing wind in Scotland is south-westerly, so you are more likely to have the wind at your back. Also, the more challenging parts are nearer to Inverness, by which time you'll be well into your stride. Finally, on average there should be less rain as you move northeast: Inverness has annual rainfall of 25 inches, compared with Fort William's 80. You may find this good for morale.

How long will it take?

Many people spread the walk over five or six days, but some take longer, depending on the time available and the pace they find comfortable. Table 1 shows distances along the Way. Don't underestimate the time you need: there is no point in being among some of Scotland's finest scenery and wildlife unless you have time to appreciate it. If you want to include side-trips and hill-walks, these may add from half a day to a couple of days to the basic walk.

Table 1	Five-day	Six-day
Fort William	🛏	🛏
	10·5	10·5
Gairlochy	🛏	🛏
	12	12
South Laggan	🛏	🛏
		10·5
Fort Augustus		🛏
	18·5	8
Invermoriston	🛏	🛏
	14	14
Drumnadrochit	🛏	🛏
	18	18
Inverness	🛏	🛏
Total	73	73

Possible overnight stops for a five- or six-day walk

Also, you need to plan how you will reach the start and return from the finish points. You may need to add an overnight in Fort William and/or Inverness depending on where you're coming from. Table 2 gives estimated times by various travel methods, and there are suggestions for combining the Way with activities other than hiking later (page 8).

Part 3 describes the Way in five sections that roughly correspond with the five map panels. This does not imply that five days is all you need: Fort Augustus is the natural half-way point, and a great place to stay. The six-day alternative in Table 1 allows a single night there. Note that both options shown above involve a long last day, and some people may prefer to split this further. If you live near the Great Glen, you could instead walk the Way in sections, for example over three week-ends, taking advantage of the regular bus service along the A82 (see page 62). Refer to the signpost at the foot of page 7 for a summary.

The overnight stops suggested in the table above reflect where services are available. Don't leave accommodation to chance: it can be scarce both out of season and in high summer, and pre-booking is essential. Specialist tour operators can organise it all for you, or you can research the options by contacting the Tourist Information Centres and relevant websites (pages 61–62). Don't leave drinking water, food or shelter to chance.

Planning your travel

To plan your travel, consult the cover maps together with the table below. There are good train and coach services to Fort William via Glasgow or Edinburgh. There are also good connections back from Inverness to Glasgow or Edinburgh, with the added option of flights from Inverness Airport to London Luton (with easyJet, see page 62) as well as to Edinburgh, Glasgow and Gatwick (British Airways).

If you are walking alone, public transport will simplify the return to your starting-point. If you are in a group with a non-walking driver, he or she can arrange to rendez-vous with hikers easily, because the A82 trunk road runs up the Great Glen. The drop-down map (back cover) shows bus stops, railway stations and main roads in more detail.

Table 2	Miles (approx)	by bus	by train	by car
Glasgow / Fort William	100	3h	3h 45m	2h 30m
Edinburgh / Fort William	145	4h	5h	3h 30m
Inverness / Fort William	70	2h	n/a	1h 30m
Inverness / Glasgow	165	4h	3h 30m	3h 30m
Inverness / Edinburgh	160	3h 30m	3h 30m	3h 30m
Glasgow / Edinburgh	45	1h	50m	45m

Distances and fastest journey times between selected places

The table above shows the fastest scheduled times for bus and train as at 2001. Car journey times are the fastest likely within speed limits, with no allowance for traffic hold-ups and minimal fuel/meal stops. All figures are rough guidelines only: contact details are given on page 62. Check schedules in advance: not all services are daily and winter timetables are often restricted.

Below and throughout, signposts show distances in miles; see page 19 for km conversion.

Fort William — 10·5 — Gairlochy — 12 — South Laggan — 10·5 — Fort Augustus — 8 — Invermoriston — 14 — Drumnadrochit — 18 — Inverness

When is the best time of year?

Fortunately for those who have little choice over their holiday dates, there is no bad time of year to walk the Way. You should be prepared for cold, wet and windy weather at any time of year; you may be lucky enough, even in winter, to experience sunshine and crisp, clear air.

However, here are a few factors to think about:

- Winter is less flexible for walkers, because the days are so much shorter: high latitude means that the hours of daylight vary from 6-7 hours in late December to 17-18 in late June.
- Winter restricts your choice of side-trips, which may be open only from April to October.
- Winter hikers are free of pests such as midges and clegs.
- On winter timetables, public transport is less frequent.
- In summer, there will be many more tourists around and heavy pressure on accommodation; however, in winter many B&Bs are closed for the season.

On balance, and if you are free to choose, the ideal months are probably May/June and September/early October. July and August are the busiest times for foreign visitors, so demand for accommodation may be heavy.

Combining the Way with other activities

There are many possibilities for combining activities. If you have two weeks to spare and like messing around with boats, you could hire a boat to sail one-way (sail or motor) and return on foot (or vice versa). There is ample scope for combining walking with golf, fishing, genealogy or leisure and many great highland hotels. Contact phone numbers and websites are given on page 62.

If you are on holiday with reluctant walkers or non-walkers, remember that the A82 is well served by buses (around six a day): stops are marked on the fold-out map. So people can join or leave your walking group along the way. If you or a group member enjoys cycling, the Great Glen Cycle Route shares various sections of the Way. On shared sections, walkers and cyclists need to be aware of each other, and cyclists should give way to walkers and cycle considerately. Cycling is not allowed on the other parts of the Way.

If you are interested in serious hill-climbing or mountaineering, there is plenty of scope (see page 30). Depending on the season, this could add significantly to your needs for equipment. Follow the Mountain Code (page 31).

The Country Code

Any long-distance route that attracts many visitors can strain the goodwill of landowners and tenant farmers. A single careless walker can spoil things for the vast majority of considerate people. Please remember that you are a guest on someone else's property. Follow the Country Code.

Be aware that the countryside provides a livelihood for its residents. Lambing takes place from February to May: never disturb pregnant ewes, nor touch young lambs, or they may be 'mis-mothered'.

> **The Country Code**
> ✓ Respect the life and work of the countryside.
> ✓ Guard against all risk of fire.
> ✓ Leave gates as you find them, open or carefully closed.
> ✓ Keep dogs under strict control.
> ✓ Keep to established footpaths, to reduce damage.
> ✓ Use gates and stiles to cross fences and walls.
> ✓ Leave livestock, crops and machinery alone.
> ✓ Take litter home.
> ✓ Help to safeguard water supplies.
> ✓ Protect wildlife, plants and trees.
> ✓ Take care on country roads.
> ✓ Avoid making unnecessary noise.

Deer stalking and game shooting take place near the Way at various times of year. These sporting activities contribute to the economy of the area, and do not affect your use of the Way. Please stick closely to the waymarked route.

 ## Dogs

Well controlled dogs are welcome on most sections, but must not be allowed to stray off the Way. However, dogs are excluded from the south-east shore of Loch Oich, as shown clearly on the map. There is a simple dog-friendly alternative: cross at Laggan Bridge and follow the Great Glen Cycle Route signs along the other shore of Loch Oich via Invergarry, rejoining the Way at Aberchalder. This exclusion is part of the agreement with the local landowner, and must be respected.

If your dog fouls the path at any time, please clear up after it. Remember also that many accommodations do not accept dogs, so check carefully before booking.

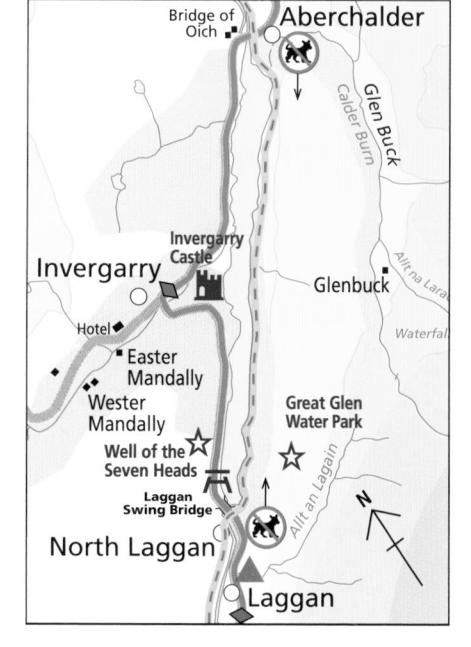

Camping and low-cost accommodation

Wild camping is not allowed anywhere on the Way. Commercial campsites generally have toilets and showers, and some have laundries. They exist along the Way near Fort William (Glen Nevis), at Gairlochy, Fort Augustus, Invermoriston, Drumnadrochit and near Inverness. Check the official website for further details (page 61).

There are youth hostels along the Way at Fort William (Glen Nevis), Loch Lochy, Loch Ness (Alltsigh) and Inverness. You neither have to be young nor to become a member to use the facilities of this registered charity (see page 62 for contact details and a useful website).

What to bring

People vary widely in what they need for comfort. Before you set limits, be clear who is carrying your overnight stuff – you or a baggage handler – and what your accommodation is – this affects whether you need to pack a towel, for example. If you are camping and can afford to offload the tent and sleeping bag onto a baggage handler, you will walk with more spring in your step. But if your budget is tight, you may have to carry everything on your back. Unless you are used to a heavy rucksack, this is strictly for the fit and experienced hiker.

If you are using B&Bs or youth hostels, don't assume that you must take a lot of extra stuff and so must rely on help with your baggage. Start by reviewing what you need to walk comfortably each day, and if the overnight extras are little more than clean underwear and a toothbrush, you may just decide to carry them and be independent of baggage handling. As of 2001, baggage handling in the Great Glen depended on local taxi firms. However, it is worth checking the official website from time to time, since baggage services akin to the excellent provision on the West Highland Way may evolve as demand grows.

In any case, think carefully about what to take and do any shopping well ahead of time. Once on the Way, shops are scarce and their supplies basic. There is no shop or bank between Fort William and Fort Augustus (although one shop is a short detour from Laggan Bridge). Likewise, between Drumnadrochit and Inverness there is no shop, pub or tearoom, so make sure you have enough to eat and drink to last for 18 fairly strenuous miles.

Notes for novices

If you've never tackled one before, the idea of a long-distance walk may seem daunting. Some people assume that it's strictly for fitness freaks, that you need years of experience or that you have to spend a fortune on special gear: wrong on all three counts. With careful planning and sensible preparation, any healthy person of any age can complete the Great Glen Way and enjoy a special sense of achievement.

Daily mileage

It is hard to predict how many miles a day you will manage comfortably. Not only do individuals vary enormously, but also the same person walks at different speeds on different terrain, or if part of a group. Some factors that affect your average speed are:

- group size and fitness
- terrain and gradient
- quality of the surroundings and the weather.

A group travels at the pace of its slowest member, or a little less. Terrain is crucial: through a peat-bog, or on loose gravel, you will walk slowly and tire more quickly. Gradient affects progress, however fit you are, and walking downhill can be surprisingly tiring. In splendid weather you may enjoy lingering, whereas in lashing rain, looking forward to a hot shower, your progress may be astonishing.

A simple rule is this: if you are walking steadily long-distance on the flat, you may average around 2½ miles per hour overall; if you are climbing or the terrain is rough, expect 2 miles per hour or even less. (These figures exclude prolonged stops, but allow for brief pauses to admire the view or take a photo.) On this basis, a 12-mile day may take around 5-6 walking hours, leaving plenty of spare time for side-trips, whereas a tough 18-mile day (eg Drumnadrochit to Inverness) could take 9 walking hours or so.

Walking the Way is different from a 'normal' holiday: you will be exercising continuously and carrying your world with you for a week. Give special thought to:

- feet
- weight
- the right gear.

Detailed notes on these are below, but you don't need to spend a lot to get started. The priorities are to buy and break in a decent pair of walking boots well in advance, and buy or borrow a rucksack. Everything else can be acquired gradually, once you're ready to have another go. Don't forget to test everything out on some day walks before you set off.

Feet

Your feet are about to become the most important part of your body. This applies especially if your normal routine involves a lot of sitting down. Unlike after weekend hiking, your feet won't have all week to recover before the next assault. Sore feet can dominate your day, your holiday and your conversation. Don't be a blister bore, or, worse still, a drop-out. Tour operators estimate that blisters are responsible for up to 95% of all drop-outs.

Some simple precautions can avoid all this. Your most important purchase is comfortable walking boots (see *The right gear* below). However good the boots, only you can 'break them in', ie let your feet and boots get used to each other. Start by wearing them around the house. Then try a half-day walk, maybe up a small hill, and if all is well test them out on progressively longer and tougher day hikes. If problems surface, take them back to the shop: better socks and insoles may help, and specialists can adjust the fit.

If you are prone to blisters, try rubbing your feet with surgical spirit (rubbing alcohol) daily for a couple of weeks before you set off on holiday. It helps to toughen the skin. Even if you've never had blisters in your life, there's always a first time. So take a pack of adhesive second-skin (see page 17). Even if you don't need it yourself, you may meet someone in agony: there is no cheaper way to make a lifelong friend.

Weight

If you are happy to travel very light, you can carry everything in your day rucksack and stay independent. If you need various luxuries for your holiday to feel familiar and enjoyable, get others to handle your baggage. However, you will still have to handle your overnight bag at the start and finish of your week, so keep its weight manageable. The less clutter you bring, the less effort you will spend on packing and unpacking. Dress among hikers is always informal.

The right gear

Boots

To buy walking boots, ideally go to a specialist outdoor/hiking shop on a weekday. Take your time over the decision: buy in haste, repent at leisure. Good shops will allow you to wear boots indoors and exchange them if they prove uncomfortable: check before you buy, and keep the receipt. Take, borrow or buy suitable socks, and remember that your feet will expand when warm: a common mistake is to buy boots that are too short. Specialist fitters can fix almost anything else about a boot, but if it is too short, they are helpless. Forget your normal shoe size; just focus on how the boot feels.

Try to test downhill walking if there is a practice slope: if your toes press against the end, the boot is too short. Ideally, the boot should have a waterproof, breathable inner layer, but this adds to the cost and may make your feet feel hotter. Don't be sidetracked by boots that seem a bargain, or look smart: the only thing that matters is whether they are comfortable. Some people find a better insole (or footbed) makes a boot feel much softer, so leave room to try this. Also, good walking socks can make a big difference: some people swear by two pairs, a thin liner sock inside a thick outer.

The main choice in boots is between the traditional leather and the modern fabric boot. The latter tend to be lighter, and may need less 'breaking in'. Tell the sales people what kind of walking you expect to do, and ask their advice.

Rucksack

The advice below refers to a simple day rucksack; if you are camping and carrying your own gear, you need a much larger, heavy-duty rucksack. Even for daytime use, buy a rucksack that's larger than you think you need: it makes for easier retrieval and packing. Around 35 litres gives plenty of room for spare clothing and water. Don't expect the rucksack to be waterproof: either buy a waterproof cover or liner, or use a bin (garbage) bag.

Check that the rucksack

- is comfortable to wear (test it heavily loaded in the shop)
- has a chest strap as well as a waist strap
- is easy to put on and take off
- has side pockets for small items
- has loops for poles (see below)
- is large enough for all you need.

Poles

If you haven't tried using poles yet, borrow one or two to try. Most people find they improve balance and reduce knee strain, especially going downhill on rough ground. They are telescopic: set them longer for downhill, shorter for uphill. Try before you buy: a pair is more efficient, especially on rough, steep terrain, but some people need a hand free for camera, binoculars or dog. However, poles are lightweight and can be stowed on your rucksack loops when not needed.

You will soon discover other uses for poles: pointing, digging mud out of boot soles, brushing brambles aside, testing the depth of flood-water, even self-defence. If you are serious about photography, consider the kind which unscrews at the top to form a camera monopod.

Clothing

The reason for needing special clothing is that your internal temperature varies so much while hiking. This is due to changes in the weather (sun, wind and rain) and in your body's heat production – rapid on an uphill climb, slower when you pause or stop.

To avoid excessive sweating, you may need to shed heat quickly. To avoid chilling, next to your body you need fabrics that 'wick' (draw away) moisture. Avoid cotton (especially denim) as it soaks up moisture (eg sweat, rainwater) and then you become cold.

To control your body temperature, use a layer system. The base layer should ideally be a synthetic 'wicking' fabric, typically polyester or specially treated cotton, eg Ventile. Over that, wear a medium-weight fleece, eg Polartec. The outer layer is a waterproof jacket and trousers; if possible, buy or borrow 'breathable' waterproofs that allow sweat to evaporate. This three-layer combination will keep you warm and dry even in a downpour and high wind. If you are lucky with the weather, the outer two layers weigh little in your rucksack.

Look for flexibility, eg trousers whose lower legs unzip to make shorts, and jackets with underarm zips. In addition, pack a warm hat and gloves: never underestimate the Scottish climate.

Water carrier

Few people carry enough water, and even fewer keep it handy. You dehydrate quickly when walking, though you may not notice it. Every time you breathe out, you lose moisture, especially when the air is cold. Top up your fluid intake as often as you can, and expect to drink two to four litres per day.

You are advised not to drink casual water without treating it. Purification tablets weigh little, and give you an unlimited safe supply. To override the slight flavour, use neutralising tablets or fruit-flavoured powder. Really strenuous walkers may be interested in isotonic drinks, ie water with added minerals to replace what you lose when sweating a lot. Isotonic powder is expensive, but you can make your own this way: mix 50% fruit juice with 50% water (drinking or treated), then add a pinch of salt and shake.

The cheapest container is a screwtop plastic bottle, worth buying because it's leakproof. However, a water bottle is of little use in the bottom of your rucksack. Try a special plastic water bag or bladder, such as a Platypus. The tube threads through your rucksack strap, so you can take a sip hands-free whenever you feel like it. That way, you drink *before* you get dehydrated.

If you are staying at a B&B, hand in your water carrier and your host will normally fill and refrigerate it overnight: just remember to collect it at breakfast. Mark your water carrier with your initials to avoid confusion.

Blister prevention and treatment

What you need is variously sold as Compeed, Moleskin or Second Skin. Use it as soon as you feel a blister coming on, or even before, to prevent one. Follow instructions carefully about warming it first and removing the backing paper. Then cover the whole area, letting it bond to the non-blistered skin. About a week later, it will fall off, by which time you will have finished your walk and forgotten the pain.

However, this miraculous stuff is useless unless you carry it in your day rucksack. Nobody develops blisters in the middle of the night.

Packing checklist

The checklist on page 18 refers to your daytime needs, and is divided into essential and desirable. Experienced walkers may disagree about what belongs in each category, but novices may appreciate a starting-point. Normally you will be wearing the first two items and carrying the rest in your rucksack.

Essential

- walking boots
- suitable clothing, including good socks
- hat, gloves and waterproofs
- water carrier and plenty of water (or purification tablets)
- food or snacks (depending on distance from next supply point)
- guidebook and maps
- blister treatment and first aid kit
- insect repellent: in summer months, expect midges (small biting insects) and/or clegs (horse-flies), notably in still weather
- waterproof rucksack cover or liner, eg bin (garbage) bag
- enough cash in pounds sterling for the week.

Cash is suggested because credit cards are not always acceptable and cash machines are not common along the Way. Bin bags have many uses, eg storing wet clothing or preventing hypothermia (cut holes for your head and arms).

Desirable

- compass, map, whistle and torch: essential if you are doing any 'serious' side-trips or hiking in winter
- pole(s)
- binoculars: useful for navigation and spotting wildlife
- camera: ideally light and rugged; remember spare batteries and film
- pouch or secure pockets: to keep small items handy but safe
- gaiters: keep trouser legs clean and dry in mud or snow
- toilet tissue (biodegradable)
- weather (sun and wind) protection for eyes and skin
- water purification tablets
- spare socks: changing socks at lunchtime can relieve damp feet
- spare shoes (eg trainers), spare bootlaces
- paper and pen.

If you are camping, you will need much more gear, including tent, groundsheet, sleeping mat and sleeping bag. You may also want a camping stove, cooking utensils and food. If you are carrying everything on your back, you will need to be strong, experienced and well-organised.

Two final, if delicate, issues: first, where should you 'go' if caught short on the Way? The official advice is

- Use public toilets where available.
- If you need to relieve yourself out of doors, pass water well away from streams, paths and bothies.
- Excrement poses health risks, and is unpleasant for others. If you have to go, choose a discreet spot at least 50 yards away from streams, paths and bothies, preferably further. If possible, bury waste in a hole six inches deep; some people carry a trowel for the purpose.

The second is what about mobile phones? You should not rely on one for personal safety: reception may be poor or non-existent. It is unfair to other people to let non-essential mobile chatter disturb the peace and the wildlife. However, if you insist on a mobile phone, be aware that coverage can be patchy. As of 2001, the best coverage is probably provided by Vodafone and Cellnet, but most networks are likely to improve their coverage over time.

Miles and kilometres, feet and metres

Distances are given mainly in miles, and heights in feet, to suit the habits of most British readers. The diagrams below are to help readers to convert between systems. The quick rule-of-thumb is:

- to convert miles to km, add 50% and round up a bit
- to convert feet to metres, divide by three and round down a bit
  In both cases the rounding error is less than 10%.

Another way of converting is to use this distance line:
British map ratios tend to be metric, with contours also shown in metres. However, mountain categories such as Munros are historically defined in feet (see pages 30-1).

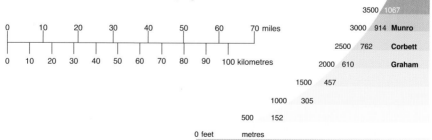

2·1 Loch Ness and the Great Glen fault

Loch Ness extends over one third of the Great Glen's length and is a major feature of the northern half of the Way. It runs from Fort Augustus almost all the way to Inverness, by way of tiny Loch Dochfour and the River Ness. Loch Ness is the centre of an area of outstanding natural beauty, with significant wildlife interest in its waters, around its shores and in its secret side glens. This section covers first the loch and its famous wildlife, then the formation of the Great Glen.

With an average depth of over 430 feet and a length of 23 miles, Loch Ness holds more water than all the lakes and reservoirs in England and Wales put together, and three times as much as Loch Lomond. Draining water from a huge area (700 square miles), it forms one of the largest freshwater systems in Europe. At its deepest point near Urquhart Castle, Loch Ness descends to 750 feet, deeper even than the North Sea. Compare this with Loch Oich, which is only 165 feet at its deepest.

Loch Ness is a massive freshwater system

Because of its great depth, Loch Ness has never been known to freeze. It is such a huge body of water that it affects the surrounding land, where snow seldom lies for very long. Most of its waters never become colder than 5° C, even after prolonged sub-zero weather. During the summer months, layers of warmer water lie above the denser colder mass, with a region of sharp temperature change called a thermocline. The water is still cold for living things, and many of its inhabitants are left over from glacial times.

What lives in Loch Ness?

It is Scotland's most famous loch mainly because of persistent reports of sightings of a monster generally known as 'Nessie'. Although Loch Morar is even deeper, plumbing depths of over 1000 feet, its alleged monster Morag has never rivalled Nessie's worldwide fame.

The monster legend dates from 565 AD when St Columba is said to have banished a creature from Loch Ness's northern end. Published reports date from 1868, when the *Inverness Courier* first mentioned the 'tradition of a huge fish gambolling in the loch'. Headlines were made by the 1933 sightings during major works on the A82, when the *Courier* again reported 'a strange spectacle on Loch Ness'.

In 1934 the the monster industry gained impetus from the publication of surgeon R K Wilson's photograph of a serpentine neck rising from a humped body. This infamous hoax was followed by hundreds of fresh photographs and thousands of sightings. Many sincere and frightened eye-witnesses described strange creatures of various shapes and sizes. Various causes have been put forward for these sightings, for example mirages and atmospheric illusions, drifting logs, boat wakes, diving birds, swimming deer, visiting seals, otter's tails and huge migrant fish.

In the 1960s the Loch Ness Investigation Bureau made systematic searches, first on the surface, then underwater, using mini-submarines and sonar. In 1987 Operation Deepscan had 20 motor cruisers sweeping the entire loch with a sonar curtain. Later, the Rosetta Project brought back long columns of sediment collected from the floor; these time capsules show how pollution and radioactivity have plumbed the depths. The scientific data collected by these investigations is stranger than the monster fiction; it is presented imaginatively by the Loch Ness 2000 experience (page 53).

Food chain in the open water of Loch Ness

Loch Ness is relatively poor in nutrients compared with, for example, Loch Lomond. Apart from the occasional migrant seal in pursuit of salmon, the top resident predator in the Loch Ness food chain is the Ferox trout. It is the large fish shown above in pursuit of a shoal of five Arctic charr, its main food source. Charr have been netted from depths of 720 feet and are relics of the ice age.

Arctic charr in turn feed directly on plankton – tiny organisms that are vital to the food chain. The creatures shown here at lower centre and right are animal plankton, less than a millimetre long (Bythotrephes and Diaptomus). Animal plankton feed on even smaller plant plankton such as those shown at top right (Tabellaria) and bottom left (Asterionella). Based on their analysis of the food chain, scientists have calculated that there just isn't enough food in the loch to sustain a resident population of very large predators.

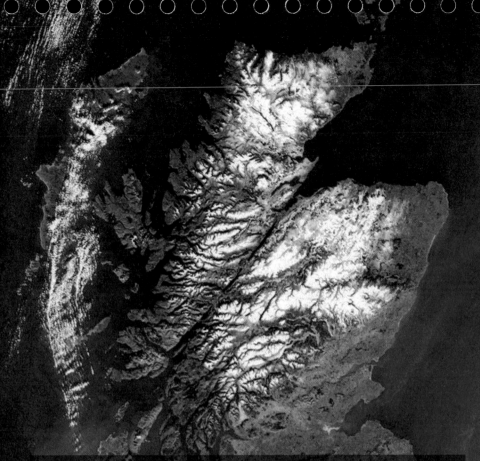

The Great Glen fault

This glen is Scotland's longest, and is known by three names: the Great Glen, Glen Mor (the Gaelic equivalent) or Glen Albyn. It is unusual in that it leads to open water at both ends, to Loch Linnhe and the Moray Firth. In effect, it joins the Atlantic Ocean to the North Sea, almost making an island of north-west Scotland.

The glen follows the line of a major geological fault created about 380 million years ago. North-west Scotland was originally joined to parts of Canada, Greenland and northern Norway. Geologists agree that there was a major upheaval around that time, although theories differ about the fault's exact formation. According to W Q Kennedy, the whole land mass was shifted and sheared 65 miles to the south-west.

In the Ice Age about 20,000 years ago, giant glaciers covered nearly all of Scotland and northern England. The ice was up to a mile thick in places, wiping out plant and animal life, and scouring a wide corridor along the line of the fault. This is still the most active area in Britain for earthquakes, with records of over 60 events, mainly very minor.

2·2 The Caledonian Canal

The geography of the Great Glen made the Caledonian Canal possible. Only 22 miles of this historic waterway are man-made, the other 38 relying on the natural waterways of Lochs Lochy, Oich and Ness. The Great Glen Way clings closely to the canal route all the way from Corpach to Fort Augustus, but does not rejoin it until the final approach to Inverness.

Its highest point is 106 feet above sea level (Loch Oich). Water drains from its southern end towards the Atlantic, and leaves its northern end towards the North Sea. Notice as you walk its length that the lock gates open in the opposite direction after the watershed. Lock gates are always angled so that the pressure of water at the higher level holds them closed.

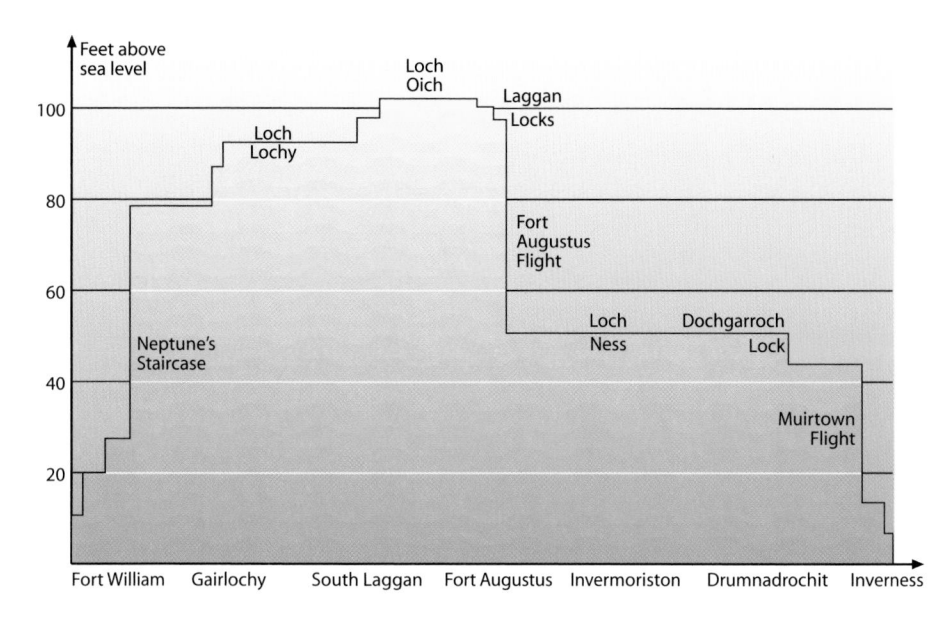

The canal was first proposed in 1773, and was designed by two engineers, William Jessop and Thomas Telford, beginning in 1803. Jessop took on Telford, the son of a Dumfries-shire shepherd, as his assistant and although they worked on it jointly, Telford seems to be given most of the credit.

It was an ambitious venture, demanding the moving of huge amounts of material and creating work for up to 1200 labourers. Telford and Jessop had proposed a canal depth of 20 feet, but dredging problems restricted the depth to around 14 feet. It took 19 years to build, and cost £912,000 - a huge sum of money at the time. There were great celebrations when it finally opened in 1822.

Although the canal was built to create jobs and boost trade, its commercial use has never been great, partly because of the depth problem. It provided a safe passage for thousands of naval vessels during the first world war, but otherwise leisure craft became its main users. It was paid for entirely by public money and remains the earliest example of nationalised transport in Britain.

Lock gates opening at Fort Augustus

The canal has 29 locks, each of which raises or lowers the level by up to eight feet. Neptune's staircase, near Fort William, is the biggest flight of locks, lifting boats 64 feet in eight closely spaced locks (page 41).

Capstans were worked by leverage

Originally locks were worked by muscle power and leverage. The lock-keeper slotted a long wooden pole into each of the four outward-facing sockets. It took seven revolutions to open or close a lock gate. The poles were stored on top of the capstan in a tall pyramid supported by the other four sockets set into the top of the capstan. Although by 1968 all the locks had been mechanised, most of the capstans have been preserved.

Cruiser heading through Kytra Lock

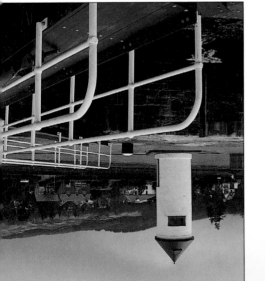

Corpach sea lock with lighthouse

The canal has many other interesting features, including ten swing bridges and various weirs, aqueducts and tunnels. There are five distinctive pepper-pot lighthouses, at Corpach, Gairlochy, Fort Augustus, where Lochs Ness and Dochfour meet, and at Inverness. Originally they were occupied and worked by lighthouse-keepers, but later all were automated.

The maximum size of ships that can navigate the canal is 35 foot beam by 150 foot long by 13.5 foot draught (or 160 foot long by 9 foot draught), and the speed limit is six miles per hour. For details of boat charters, operating hours and regulations, see page 62.

2·3 Historical background

Some ten hill-top forts testify to the Great Glen's strategic importance since the Iron Age. These may have formed a line-of-sight signalling system using beacons. The most interesting forts that are accessible to Wayfarers include Torr Dhuin (from Fort Augustus), Urquhart Castle (Drumnadrochit) and Craig Phadrig (from Inverness). Dun Deardail is a small diversion off the West Highland Way south of Fort William.

View to the north from Craig Phadrig

Radioactive carbon dating suggests that Craig Phadrig was constructed around 350 BC. Although destroyed soon after it was built, this site was occupied afterwards from time to time up to about 400 AD. It sometimes takes imagination and background knowledge to make sense of what you can see at ground level, but these forts are worth visiting if only for the glorious views from their hill-top sites.

The tower of Urquhart Castle

These forts are called vitrified (glassy) because of the shiny appearance of their stones after intense fires had partly melted them. Mystery surrounds the cause of these fires, whether deliberate or accidental, but they must have burned for long periods at extremely high temperatures.

Many more recent historic sites are referred to in Part 3, often arising from feuds between rival clans. In the 12th and 13th centuries, castles were built at Urquhart, Invergarry and Inverlochy (Fort William). The next section explains the background to the Jacobite risings in the early 18th century and how this led to the military road system and the barracks at Fort William, Fort Augustus and Fort George (page 59).

The Jacobite risings and General Wade

In 1688, James VII of Scotland (who was also James II of England) was deposed by popular demand, partly because he was thought to be promoting the Catholic Church. Parliament chose instead his daughter Mary, also of the house of Stewart, who had married the Dutch Protestant William of Orange.

After William and Mary came to the British throne (1688-9), those who supported the other Stewart line of James VII and his son James (the 'Old Pretender') became known as Jacobites: Jacobus is Latin for James. Queen Mary showed little interest in Scotland and her Dutch husband, William of Orange, was resented as a foreigner. The unpopularity of the 1707 Act of Union, together with the sense of distance from decisions made in London, gave the Jacobite cause a nationalist flavour.

During 1689-1745, contact was kept up between Scotland and the Jacobite court, first in France then Italy. The two famous Jacobite risings took place in 1715 and 1745. The 'Fifteen' focused on the Old Pretender, and the 'Forty-five' on his son, Charles Edward Stewart, also known as 'Bonnie Prince Charlie' or the 'Young Pretender'.

In 1746, the Battle of Culloden (see page 59) marked the final defeat of the Jacobites. Against advice, Bonnie Prince Charlie insisted on pitched battle on an open site unsuited to his highlanders' tactics. His army was hungry, sleepless and heavily outnumbered, and government troops led by 'Butcher' Cumberland routed them in under an hour. About 2000 Jacobites were killed in this battle, the last fought on British soil. However, 'Bonnie Prince Charlie' remained in Scotland for another five months, living in hiding, being pursued all over the highlands and islands by the military.

General George Wade (1673-1748) was an Irishman who served as Commander-in-Chief of the army in North Britain (Scotland) from 1724-40. During that period, he built 240 miles of military roads in the highlands, including roads along the southern banks of Lochs Oich and Ness (1725-6). He helped to plan the barracks at Fort Augustus (completed in 1742).

Many of the works credited to Wade were actually built by William Caulfeild, who had been his deputy and was in charge from 1740-67. Wade and Caulfeild built roads to a standard width of six feet, with drainage ditches on either side. Wade's work is referred to as 'crushing rebellious Scots' in one (seldom sung) verse of Britain's national anthem.

The Corrieyairack Pass from Meall a' Cholumain

Wade's legacy includes many miles of roads and bridges which survive and are used by hikers 250 years later. His road through the Corrieyairack Pass south of Fort Augustus was built by 500 soldiers in 1731, and for over a century it was the highest maintained public road in Britain.

The Great Glen has pre-historic evidence of human habitation, notably Clava Cairns (page 59), with its two passage graves and a ring cairn. Although previously thought to be neolithic, recent radio carbon dating shows a range of dates from 2500-2000 BC, with re-use in the late Bronze Age.

Clava Cairns, a well-preserved Bronze Age site

2·4 Munros, Corbetts and Grahams

A Munro is a Scottish mountain whose summit is over 3000 feet (914 m) in height, provided its peak is not too close to a neighbouring Munro, when it may be classified as a mere 'Top'.

They are named after Hugh Munro, a London-born doctor (1856-1919). His published table (1891) listed 238 such peaks (and 538 Tops). There has been protracted debate about the exact total, and the distinction between a summit and a Top, ever since. The Scottish Mountaineering Club's 1997 figure is 284 Munros and 511 Tops, the revised numbers reflecting more accurate survey methods.

The first 'Munroist' was the Reverend A E Robertson, who completed his final Munro (as then listed) in 1901. Since then, 'Munro-bagging' has become a popular sport. The list has changed to include the notorious 'Inaccessible Pinnacle' in Skye.

Some determined climbers ascend all the Munros in a single expedition lasting several months, whereas others spread the challenge over a lifetime. Charlie Campbell, a Glasgow postman, set a most impressive record of 48½ days in July 2000. At least 100 people become Munroists every year, and thousands of people are working on their personal lists as you read this.

Looking toward Loch Ness from the summit of Ben Tee

The Way begins near Ben Nevis (4406 feet, 1344 m), the highest mountain in Britain. Many other fine mountains are accessible from the Fort William area. Two Munros are reached easily from Laggan Locks: Sron a' Choire Ghairbh (3074 feet, 937 m) and Meall na Teanga (3012 feet, 918 m).

A Corbett is smaller: over 2500 feet (762 m) and with a drop of at least 500 feet all round. There are seven Corbetts close to the Way, including Ben Tee (2966 feet, 904 m) from whose summit there is a panoramic view (page 30).

A Graham is smaller again, and is defined metrically as over 610 m (2001 feet) and with a drop of at least 150 m (492 feet) all round. There are five Grahams close to the Way, including Meall Fuar-mhonaidh (2293 feet, 699 m) which you can climb from Grotaig (page 52) and which gives splendid views over Loch Ness.

Meall Fuar-mhonaidh, overlooking Loch Ness

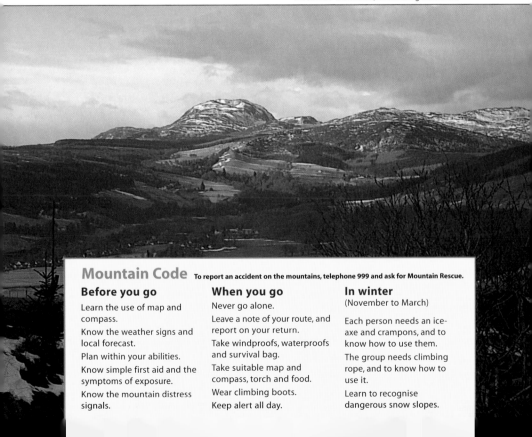

Mountain Code To report an accident on the mountains, telephone 999 and ask for Mountain Rescue.

Before you go

Learn the use of map and compass.

Know the weather signs and local forecast.

Plan within your abilities.

Know simple first aid and the symptoms of exposure.

Know the mountain distress signals.

When you go

Never go alone.

Leave a note of your route, and report on your return.

Take windproofs, waterproofs and survival bag.

Take suitable map and compass, torch and food.

Wear climbing boots.

Keep alert all day.

In winter
(November to March)

Each person needs an ice-axe and crampons, and to know how to use them.

The group needs climbing rope, and to know how to use it.

Learn to recognise dangerous snow slopes.

2·5 Habitats and wildlife

Salmon leaping upstream

The Great Glen Way runs through three main types of habitat, described below:

- water-side
- woodland
- heath and moorland.

If you are really keen to spot wildlife, carry binoculars and walk alone, or seek fellow-walkers who share your interest and are willing to keep quiet when it matters. Try to set off soon after sunrise, or go for a stroll in the evening. Animals are much more active at these times than in the middle of the day. Since this applies to midges too, protect your skin thoroughly, especially from May to September and in still weather.

Water-side

Oystercatcher

Much of the Way lies near water, along man-made canal or various lochs and rivers. Look out for insects, birds and perhaps some mammals.

Near Corpach, look for oystercatchers in the fields. Their strong orange bills are good at cracking open cockles and mussels, and they are easy to spot: look for the white-on-black M-shape in flight and listen for their piercing cries.

You are likely to see Britain's most widespread bird of prey, the kestrel. It feeds on small mammals, mainly field voles and mice: its excellent eyesight lets it detect their tiny movements in the grass, and it hunts in a fast dive with half-closed wings. Recognise it by its ability to hover and its pointed chestnut-coloured wings.

Because the Great Glen is open to the sea at both ends, some sea birds use it as a corridor. You may see wandering seabirds such as kittiwakes, guillemots, fulmars and shearwaters in the heart of the glen. Look for cormorants hanging out their wings to dry, especially at Invermoriston pier. For wildlife in Loch Ness, see page 22; keep a look-out for anything unexpected on or in the water.

Look out for grey heron hunting for fish and frogs: sometimes they stand tall and motionless in the shallows, at other times they stalk their prey. In flight, they trail their legs and their huge grey wings beat very slowly.

If you are very lucky, you might see the magnificent osprey diving talons first to carry off a fish. Rescued from extinction in Britain, the osprey population has slowly grown in the highlands since the first pair returned to Loch Garten in 1955. They are visitors, over-wintering in West Africa and returning each spring, often to the same nesting site. Ospreys established three new nest sites in the Great Glen during 1998-2001.

Osprey lifting its prey out of the loch torpedo-style

Pine martens depend on woodland habitats

Woodland

The Great Glen is richly wooded, with a mixture of native species (broad-leaved and pine) and productive conifers. These woodlands also provide food, nesting sites and shelter for wildlife.

In prehistoric times, Scotland was covered by natural mixed woodlands known as the ancient Caledonian forest. On the lower and south-facing slopes, birch, oak, ash, cherry, hazel and rowan flourished. Birch were also successful on the higher ground, along with Scots pine, juniper and other hardy species. In the wetter areas, willow and alder predominated.

Over the last 4000-5000 years, humans cleared this forest to make way for crops, animal grazing or the planting of other tree species. However, remnants of the Caledonian forest survive and you still see ancient oakwoods, for example on the slopes of Loch Ness. Native pinewoods support many rare birds, including crested tit, Scottish crossbill and siskin (foot of page 35).

The pine marten became almost extinct in Britain and is therefore protected. Its rapid population rise in the Great Glen reflects the increase in woodland. It is the only predator agile enough to catch red squirrels.

Crested tit perching on Scots pine

Look for wood ants and their huge nests in the forest above Loch Ness near Grotaig. Tread carefully and please do not disturb them, as they occupy a niche in the food chain.

The productive forests in the Great Glen are dominated by non-native species, eg Douglas fir, Norway spruce, lodgepole pine and larch (European, Japanese and hybrid). These woods are an important habitat: big birds such as osprey, buzzard and goshawk need big trees in which to nest.

Douglas fir is a valuable timber crop

The Forestry Commission (FC) owns most of the forests that you walk through, and enlightened planting policies have made for more diversity, not only in species, but also in the age structure of the tree population, with clear felling sometimes avoided, and two trees planted for every one felled. There is a target of 20% open space in newly planted areas. These policies are aimed at supporting all the wildlife niches in a sustainable way.

Sometimes the FC takes a more active role in conservation. Scotland has 75% of the British red squirrel population, but on the south side of Loch Ness squirrels were being run over when crossing the road. The FC solution was to suspend bridges of thick rope 16 feet high above the roads, and grateful squirrels now use these rope bridges.

Red squirrel on rope bridge; siskin (inset)

Three kinds of deer live in woodland, of which only red and roe deer are native. Sika deer were introduced into deer parks from Japan as recently as 1870; some escaped and bred successfully in the highlands, despite the harsh climate. They are difficult to spot because they stand motionless when frightened and prefer dense woodland. During the rut, sika stags make an eerie whistling noise.

Heath and moorland

Examples of Scots pine are found in this peaty moorland. After the Ice Age, 8 to 10 thousand years ago, Scots pine re-colonised the Great Glen; it is the only pine tree native to Britain. Isolated trees are useful perches for birds of prey.

Sika deer browse on Norway spruce

Look up and you may see kestrel, buzzard or merlin. Birds of prey such as owls depend on small mammals for their diet. The field vole lives on grass, plants and fruit, and eight different birds prey on it. As much as 90% of the barn owl's diet consists of field voles.

Field vole feeding on an apple

Mature Scots pine has a distinctive shape

Buzzards are much larger than owls, and are also known as 'the tourist's eagle', because visitors so often mistake them for eagle. The golden eagle's wing-span is over six feet, double the buzzard's, and it is confined to more remote areas: consider yourself very lucky if you see one.

Skylarks have suffered badly on farmland elsewhere, but they flourish in the Great Glen. If you hear a call like the whistle of a boiling kettle, look for curlew, which has a long curved bill. On higher ground, watch and listen for grouse (red and black). You might see ptarmigan, a mountain grouse whose body feathers turn white in winter.

If you see pathways of nibbled heather and blaeberry, look for mountain hare, which also turns white in winter. Even in their brown coats, the mountain hare looks different from its brown

Mountain hare

cousin: its ears are much shorter and its tail lacks the black tip. Hare predators include the fox and golden eagle; there are very few rabbits in the Great Glen. A healthy population of mountain hare may help eagles to sustain two chicks per year. The heather thus almost directly supports the golden eagle that soars above it.

Owls prey on voles and mice

37

3·1 The starting-point: Fort William

Originally called Inverlochy, the town had a crude fort built in 1654-5 by General Monk. This was replaced by a stone fort in 1690, when the town was renamed after William III (William of Orange). It is a centre for tourism and shopping in the west highlands, and a good base for hikers and climbers.

- Although the Fort withstood many conflicts, in 1890 the railway was built over it, and little has survived. Look for traces opposite the railway station and supermarket car park, on the banks of Loch Lochy.
- Many mountains are nearby, including Ben Nevis, Britain's highest (see page 31). Glen Nevis offers superb hiking, with its waterfalls, its precarious three-string bridge and a wealth of wild flowers and birds. Its Visitor Centre is open daily from Easter to late October (tel 01397 705 922).
- The town's West Highland Museum has information about the town and its fortifications: open year-round Monday to Saturday, also on Sunday afternoons in July/August (tel 01397 702 169).
- Climb Cow Hill (942 ft) for splendid views over mountains and lochs. Pick out the line of the river Lochy and Caledonian Canal leading northeast to Loch Lochy along the Great Glen.
- Two miles northeast of the town on the A82, the Ben Nevis distillery has a visitor centre, offers tours and tastings, and is open Monday to Saturday, Easter to October (tel 01397 700 200).

Fort William (foreground) with Ben Nevis behind

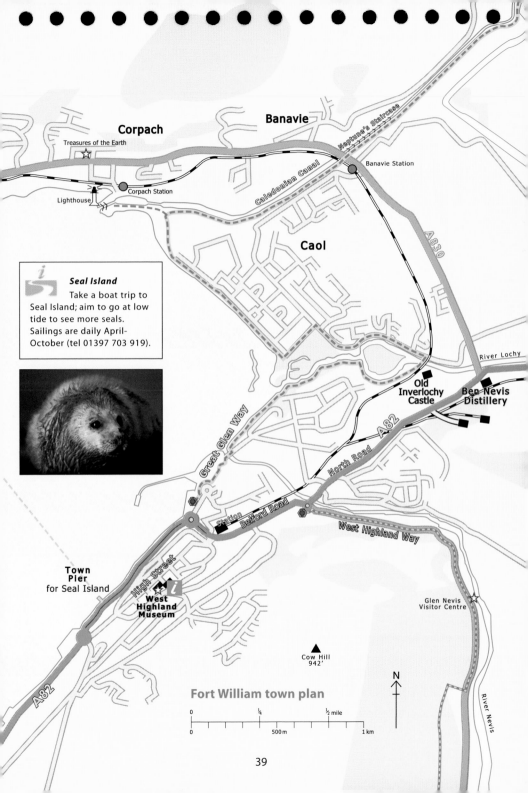

Corpach

Treasures of the Earth ☆

Corpach Station

Lighthouse

Banavie

Neptune's Staircase

Banavie Station

Caledonian Canal

Caol

A830

River Lochy

Old Inverlochy Castle

Ben Nevis Distillery

Great Glen Way

A82

North Road

West Highland Way

Station

Belford Road

Town Pier
for Seal Island

High Street

☆ **West Highland Museum**

Glen Nevis Visitor Centre ☆

A82

River Nevis

▲ Cow Hill
942'

N
↑

Fort William town plan

| 0 | ¼ | ½ mile |
| 0 | 500 m | 1 km |

> *i*
> *Seal Island*
>   Take a boat trip to Seal Island; aim to go at low tide to see more seals. Sailings are daily April-October (tel 01397 703 919).

3·2 Fort William to Gairlochy

Map	panel 3.2 (outside back cover)
Distance	10.5 miles (17 km)
Terrain	pavement at first, then riverside path, more pavement, remainder canal towpath
Grade	very easy
Food and drink	Fort William, Caol, Banavie, Gairlochy (seasonal)
Side-trips	Old Inverlochy Castle, Corpach sea lock, Treasures of the Earth
Summary	flat walking, with many interesting canal features, including Neptune's Staircase, and views of Ben Nevis

- Follow the waymarkers from the official start, heading north-west out of Fort William. Refer to the town plan on page 39 as needed. Just before you cross the River Lochy, it's worth visiting Old Inverlochy Castle.

- After the Castle, head back towards the sea loch and follow the shoreline path to the Caledonian Canal. Instead of following the Way by turning right, turn left for a short diversion to Corpach sea lock, with its lock-keepers' cottages and pepper-pot lighthouse (pages 26 and 40).

- The sea lock is close to Treasures of the Earth, a superb collection of gemstones and crystals, displayed in caves and mining scenes: open daily (tel 01397 772 283). Once back on the towpath, follow it all the way to Gairlochy. At Banavie (**Bann**avee), notice Neptune's Staircase (page 25).

- From Banavie to Gairlochy, enjoy the increasingly rural walk with a fine variety of trees and good views of the mountains on each side of the glen. Notice four splendid aqueducts in this section, and consider a short diversion to see the ruins of Torcastle, which overlooks the pretty River Lochy.

- Shortly you reach the historic swing bridge of Moy: each half has to be opened separately. Soon after, you arrive at the small village of Gairlochy.

Old Inverlochy Castle

Old Inverlochy Castle is one of Scotland's earliest stone castles, built by Sir John Comyn, Black Lord of Badenoch. The site had been fortified since AD 273. The castle was built in 1260 as a square with 9-foot thick walls and a round tower at each corner. Open daily year-round.

Neptune's Staircase

Fort William — 4.5 — Banavie — 6 — Gairlochy

Looking towards Laggan Locks from above Kilfinnan

3.3 Gairlochy to South Laggan

Map	panels 3.2 and 3.3 (outside back cover)
Distance	12 miles (19 km)
Terrain	a mix of tarmac and forest paths and tracks, mostly shared with the Great Glen Cycle Route
Grade	easy
Food and drink	Gairlochy (seasonal), Great Glen Water Park (Loch Oich-side)
Side-trips	Clan Cameron Museum (Achnacarry)/Cia-aig waterfall
Summary	fairly easy walking along the length of Loch Lochy, with splendid views

Clan Cameron Museum, Achnacarry

- In this section, you walk through land owned by the Camerons of Lochiel. Two miles after Gairlochy, there is the option of a small diversion to their museum, which you can combine with visiting the Cia-aig (pronounced Kaig) waterfall to rejoin the Way at Clunes. Bonnie Prince Charlie hid in a cave here for two weeks after his flight from Culloden.

- Achnacarry House has belonged to the Camerons since 1660, but was destroyed in 1746 to punish them for their role in the Jacobite rising. This was the last place where clan chiefs used the pit and gallows to punish cattle stealers. The House was damaged in the second world war but was rebuilt afterwards.

The Clan Cameron Museum covers the history of the clan and its Jacobite links, and has also photographs and reminders from the commando training era. It is open afternoons daily from April to October, also late mornings in July/August (tel 01397 712 480). Continue past the museum and cross the white bridge to reach the tip of Loch Arkaig. Turn right along the B8005 and near the hump-backed bridge look for where the waters of the Cia-aig fall into the Witch's Cauldron. Return along the Dark Mile (Mile Dorcha) to Clunes.

- Allow an extra 2-3 hours for this option, but spare a thought for the Commando recruits who in wartime, heavily laden, had to complete the five-mile round trip in under 50 minutes. From 1942-45, Achnacarry housed the British Commando Basic Training Centre, which put 25,000 recruits through an extremely tough training system. Some recruits died because of a realistic regime that used live ammunition; the memorial at Spean Bridge honours their memory (page 44).

Gairlochy — South Laggan

12

Loch Lochy

- From Clunes all the way to Kilfinnan, you walk on forest tracks, punctuated by splendid views of Loch Lochy with the mountains behind. You pass Glas-dhoire, a ruined bothy, and reach the cemetery at Kilfinnan with a large mausoleum for the chiefs of Glengarry. Be aware that most of this section is shared with the Cycle Route.

- The last section from Kilfinnan to Laggan Locks is on a minor road. You are close to the site of the Battle of the Shirts in July 1544. This was a clan battle between the Frasers on one side and the ranks of Camerons, MacDonalds and MacDonnells on the other. It acquired its strange name from the unusually hot weather: such was the blazing sunshine that the men removed their plaids and fought wearing only undershirts.

Commando memorial, Spean Bridge

- Laggan has a Youth Hostel, but as of 2001 no refreshments. A mile further on, the Great Glen Water Park has a coffee shop and restaurant, provides accommodation (mainly by the week) and offers a wide range of water sports and other activities (telephone 01809 501 381).

- Enjoy the fine views westward towards two nearby Munros. To climb either, you need suitable equipment and experience (page 31). You take the high track through South Laggan Forest south-west from Kilfinnan, striking west just above Glas-dhoire to follow the Allt Glas Dhoire upstream to the summit of the pass (Cam Bhealach). From there, you can reach either Sron a' Choire Ghairbh or Meall na Teanga. However, mist can descend suddenly, so be prepared to use your compass and detailed map.

3·4 South Laggan to Invermoriston

Map	**panels 3.3 and 3.4 (outside and inside back cover)**
Distance	**18.5 miles (30 km)**
Terrain	**some tarmac, railway track-bed, old military road, then canal towpath to Fort Augustus; afterwards forest track almost to Invermoriston (beware bicycles)**
Grade	**easy to Fort Augustus; noticeable gradients thereafter**
Food and drink	**Great Glen Water Park, Fort Augustus, Invermoriston**
Side-trips	**Meall a' Cholumain (from Fort Augustus), Fort Augustus (various)**
Summary	**scenic sections along Loch Oich-side and past Kytra Lock, with mixed woodland and lovely views; break this section overnight in the Fort Augustus area if time**

- From South Laggan to Aberchalder, you walk along the canalside through the tall trees of Laggan Avenue and near a small stone church, both established by Thomas Telford. At Laggan swing bridge, you have the option of a diversion to visit the macabre Well of the Seven Heads or to buy groceries at the shop. Otherwise, carry on past the Great Glen Water Park and into the Leiterfearn nature reserve and enjoy the wonderful ash, elm and hazel woodland.

- At the start of the forest you may notice a wall, a relic of old Invergarry station, a stop on the ill-fated railway whose trackbed you now pick up. Trains used to run between Spean Bridge and Fort Augustus, but the line was abandoned in 1911, a casualty of rivalry and treachery between competing railway companies. Although it was briefly reprieved by popular demand, it finally closed in 1946.

- Looking west across Loch Oich you may glimpse the ruins of Invergarry Castle, once the seat of the MacDonnells. Like many of the Great Glen clans, they supported the Jacobite cause. Bonnie Prince Charlie stayed there twice, and the castle was burned after Culloden.

At Aberchalder, notice the splendid old Bridge of Oich, designed by James Dredge in 1850, which carried cars until 1932. Its double-cantilevered chains taper elegantly towards the middle, and are suspended between granite arches.

The gentle descent from Aberchalder to Fort Augustus is perhaps the most secluded stretch of canal, past the delightful Kytra Lock (page 26) and through splendid mixed woodland. Often you are walking along a narrow causeway, the canal to your right and the river, more often heard than seen, to your left.

Before Kytra, the canal broadens into a natural narrow loch, with no embankment on its east side. To the east, look up for the television mast marking the summit of Meall a' Cholumain. This modest climb from Fort Augustus is rewarded by spectacular views over the lochs to the south-west and the Corrieyairack Pass to the east. The photographs on pages 47 and 29 were both taken from this vantage point.

Well of the Seven Heads

This monument was put up in 1812 as a reminder of a gruesome clan massacre in 1663. Following a dispute with the MacDonnells over succession, two Keppochs were killed, allegedly by accident. In retaliation, the Keppochs killed seven MacDonnells, allegedly the murderers, in their own homes. Their severed heads were taken to a Glengarry chief, who is said to have washed them here.

River Oich at Fort Augustus

Fort Augustus

Originally known as Kilcumein, the village was renamed in 1729 by General Wade in honour of William Augustus, Duke of Cumberland. Midway between Fort William and Fort George, Fort Augustus was built in 1729 and became the hub of Wade's network of military roads.

The fort housed troops long after Culloden, but in 1867 it was sold to Lord Lovat (a descendant of an executed Jacobite). He gave it to Benedictine monks who used it as a monastery, a school and then an abbey (1882-1998). After the abbey closed the monks moved to Pluscarden, and in 2001 it was still unclear in what form it might re-open.

The locks, Fort Augustus

Fort Augustus has many attractions, notably the sight of boats working through the flight of five locks at its centre. Visit the Caledonian Canal Heritage Centre, on the west side of the canal (Ardchattan House, tel 01320 366 493). There is also the Clansman Centre on its east side, with living history museum, craft shop and armoury (01320 366 444).

You can also cruise Loch Ness with sonar from here, from March to November; contact Cruise Loch Ness at 01320 366 221. The Forestry Commission has leaflets with forest walks, including one to the Iron Age hilltop fort of Torr Dhuin (page 27).

The view south-west from Meall a'Cholumain

The falls of Moriston

- You climb steeply out of Fort Augustus through a forest of birch and pine, with good views back over the town with its locks and abbey. Note that Loch Ness's only 'island' below you is actually a man-made crannog. Originally called Eilean Muireach, it was renamed Cherry Island by Oliver Cromwell. Its trees are tall pines; the name refers only to its circular shape.

- A crannog is an artifical Iron Age island made by piling up stones on the loch bed to make a foundation for a timber house, often on wooden stilts, so as to be secure from enemies. This one was identified only in 1908 when an intrepid Benedictine monk from Fort Augustus Abbey explored it, using diving gear borrowed from Canal workers.

- This section is mainly through conifers, but notice the wide variety of species and ages. From time to time you have dramatic views across Loch Ness through the gaps in the forest. Within a few miles you reach the tiny village of Invermoriston. The River Moriston brings water from the high ground of Kintail, tumbling into Loch Ness through spectacular rocks near the splendid old bridge.

- The old bridge at Invermoriston was designed by Thomas Telford. It was begun in 1805, one of a thousand built in the early 19th century. Its design was sound enough, but there were problems both with its construction and spiralling costs. The businessman who financed it was bankrupt before its completion in 1813.
- The bridge was restored many times, but after flood damage in 1951, it was replaced by the modern bridge (1954). This gives a good vantage point for admiring the old Telford bridge.
- Glen Moriston timber has had economic value since the 13th century when ships were built from its oak and pine to go on the Crusades. Much later, trees were also floated downstream for use in constructing the Caledonian Canal. Hydro-electric power is produced by the Dundreggan dam and power station.

The old bridge at Invermoriston

3.5 Invermoriston to Drumnadrochit

Map	panels 3.4 and 3.5 (inside back cover)
Distance	14 miles (22 km)
Terrain	mainly forest tracks, last section following line of minor road with off-road footpath in places
Grade	mainly moderate with some steep sections
Food and drink	none between Invermoriston and Drumnadrochit
Side-trips	Urquhart Castle, Loch Ness Visitor Centres (two), Loch Ness cruises (various), Drum Farm Centre
Summary	fine high-level forest section with superb views over Loch Ness

Urquhart Castle, Loch Ness

Urquhart Castle

- Urquhart (pronounced **Urk**hurt) enjoys one of the most majestic situations of any castle in Scotland. From Strone Point these splendid ruins command fine views along Loch Ness in both directions. It was built on an Iron Age fortress site around 1250 for Alan Durward, Lord of Urquhart and son-in-law of King Alexander II. The castle was taken from the English by William Wallace at the end of the 13th century, but Edward I's soldiers recaptured it afer a long siege in 1303.

- The castle changed hands many times in the 14th and 15th centuries and was besieged twice in the 16th by the Macdonald Lords of the Isles. It was disputed by the Jacobites in 1689, and partly blown up by government troops when they left in 1692. Sadly it was never repaired and much of its stone, timber and lead was plundered as building material.

- Many of the present buildings are 17th century onward, although some earlier parts survive and Pictish remains suggest a much earlier use of this site. The castle was used as a fortress and a residence for over 400 years. Its best preserved part is the five-storey tower house which dates from the 16th century (page 27).

- The castle draws about 250,000 tourists per annum, the majority in the summer months. To enjoy the castle without the crowds, time your visit carefully. Completion of a £4 million visitor centre and site upgrade was due by autumn 2001. The castle is maintained by Historic Scotland and opens daily throughout the year (telephone 01456 450 551).

Invermoriston   **Drumnadrochit**

14

Loch Ness

Meall Fuar-mhonaidh, a distinctive landmark

Invermoriston to Drumnadrochit step-by-step

- The shoreline of Loch Ness is generally very steep and, combined with wind and waves, presents problems for plant and animal life. Flatter land is more hospitable, so be alert for more wildlife in these areas. There is an important area of alder swamp, a Site of Special Scientific Interest (SSSI), near where the Rivers Enrick and Coiltie drain into Urquhart Bay.

- You begin with a steep climb out of Invermoriston and for much of the walk you are on forest tracks, often high above the water and with splendid views. The forest has a hidden interest, with trees surrounding a fine old packhorse bridge near where you cross the Allt Saigh river.

- At Grotaig, you pass near to another of the Great Glen's Iron Age forts, Dun Scriben. Keen hillwalkers may wish to climb Meall Fuar-mhonaidh from here (see page 31). Pronounced (roughly) Fur**vann**ie, its distinctive rounded summit is a landmark for many miles around.

- You follow the minor road for several miles along the hillside. Looking down on the water on a still day, you can imagine why John Cobb chose this spot for his attempt on the water speed record. There is a memorial on the A82 to his death in 1952 in the attempt.

- You leave the minor road to descend to the River Coiltie, then walk along the riverside into Lewiston, turning left along the main road into Drumnadrochit.

Looking towards Grotaig from across Loch Ness

Drumnadrochit

- Drumnadrochit (almost rhymes with rocket) is locally known as 'Drum'. Combined with neighbouring Lewiston, its population is about 1500. Although a smallish place, it hosts a number of visitor attractions. A new Tourist Information Centre opened in May 2001 in the village centre.

- Drum is the capital of the monster industry: its two Loch Ness visitor centres are oddly labelled 'official' and 'original'. Don't be put off by the floating Nessie model in the lochan outside the 'official' Loch Ness 2000: be sure to visit it (open daily, telephone 01456 450 573). You walk through six themed areas that present multimedia findings from the explorations, letting you judge for yourself. It attracts 200,000 visitors per annum and houses a field centre with educational and scientific goals. The project supports an informative website (page 62). There are loch cruises, and the complex includes shops and a hotel.

- The 'original' Loch Ness Visitor Centre shows a film, has an exhibition and also offers loch cruises (telephone 01456 450 342). Also in the village centre is Castle Cruises (Art Gallery, telephone 01456 450 695) and the Drum Farm Centre with many family attractions and a tearoom – open Monday to Saturday, April to October (telephone 01456 450 788).

The mysterious deep waters of Loch Ness

River Ness

3.6 Drummadrochit to Inverness

Map	panels 3.5 and 3.6 (inside back cover)
Distance	18 miles (29 km)
Terrain	mainly forest and moorland tracks, with several miles on a minor road and finally pavements
Grade	mainly moderate, steep leaving Drummadrochit, and a significant descent into Inverness
Food and drink	none between Drummadrochit and Inverness
Summary	the most challenging section of the Way, with some spectacular views, finishing at Inverness Castle

- This is the most challenging day's walking, and perhaps also the most varied, with a mixture of farmland, exposed high moorland and farm and woodland, finishing on the bustling pavements of Inverness.

- You leave Drumnadrochit alongside the busy A82, but within two miles you start to climb above it at Tychat (pronounced with a long **y**). Over the next couple of miles you contour the shoulders of Meall na h-Eilrig. Look back for your last views over Urquhart Castle and the loch beyond. To the south-west you may see the landmark of Meall Fuar-mhonaidh.

- Near Achpopuli (pronounced Ach**pop**youlee) you pick up a forest track which passes near Loch Laide, famous for its very pure water. You are a mile above the settlement of Abriachan (Ab**ree**achan), the tiny centre of Britain's largest community forest. In 1995 the Abriachan Forest Trust bought 403 acres of woodland from the Forestry Commission, and with strong local participation manages it for wildlife and community benefit, creating marked trails, newsletters and a book.

- Two miles after Achpopuli, the Way picks up the minor road from Abriachan to Blackfold. It's worth turning sharp right instead, for a 500-yard diversion to see the Caiplich prehistoric settlement and field system. You may be able to pick out several hut circles which are over 2000 years old. The local community took the initiative in clearing access to this scheduled ancient monument. Retrace your steps to resume the Way.

- As the road descends to Blackfold, you start to be aware of the Great Glen again, but Loch Ness has given way to tiny Loch Dochfour and the River Ness, which are out of sight. After Blackfold you walk through Craig Leach forest, mainly pine but with wide paths and plenty of light and shade.

- After a while, you gain your first glimpse of water to the north: this is the Beauly Firth, which meets the Moray Firth at Inverness, the first sign of your destination.

- You pass Dunain Hill to your right, now walking though mixed broadleaved trees. Passing close to Leachkin chambered cairn, look north for the hill on which Craig Phadrig stands (page 59). The Way approaches Inverness from the west, crossing open ground near the golf course and two hospitals, then across playing fields until you reach the Caledonian Canal for the first time since Fort Augustus.

- Refer to the plan on page 60, remembering that its north is straight up the page, whereas the drop-down map has its north rotated. (The aerial photograph on page 57 also looks north, with the Kessock bridge just visible at its upper right.)

- Cross the canal and turn right to follow Bught Road until you cross the river by way of Ness Islands. On the east bank, you soon pass the Infirmary Footbridge, named after the Royal Northern Infirmary, which has several listed buildings. From there it is a small step to your final destination, Inverness castle.

The Infirmary Footbridge, Inverness

- The site of Inverness has been inhabited for at least 7000 years, and is full of historic and pre-historic interest. Neolithic stone circles and passage-type burial cairns have been found in and around the town. Long regarded as the 'capital of the highlands', Inverness became Scotland's newest city in 2001.

- The modern town has good communications by rail, water, air and road, and features the Kessock suspension bridge (opened in 1982) which takes the A9 northward across the Beauly Firth. Its mainly nineteenth century public buildings are evidence of the expansion resulting from earlier advances in communication, the arrival of the railways and the building of the Caledonian Canal.

- St Andrew's Cathedral stands beside the River Ness, and its twin towers are a distinctive landmark. It was founded by Bishop Eden, but designed by the town's Provost, Alexander Ross. Work began in 1866 and within three years it had reached almost its present form. Ross had intended 200-foot spires to complete the towers, but they were abandoned because of rising costs.

St Andrew's Cathedral

- The Castle was built on the site of a much older royal castle. By 1718 it had a large tower house, bastioned by General Wade, and a court-house was added in 1843. Part of it was originally a prison but later became a sheriff court. A Castle Garrison Encounter is staged daily except Sundays, from March to November (telephone 01463 243 363).

Inverness Castle

- The museum and art gallery stands in Castle Wynd. It has displays on the Great Glen, the Caledonian Canal and highland heritage and folk life, including Jacobite tartans and other costumes. It is open daily except Sundays, year-round (telephone 01463 237 114).

- The Eden Court Theatre is a multi-purpose complex with an 800-seat theatre, a conference centre and an art gallery. Telephone 01463 234 234 for a free guide to events year-round.

- Two miles north-west of Inverness town centre, the Caledonian Canal finally reaches open water. Complete your 'coast-to-coast' journey by visiting Clachnaharry, where the sea lock had to be built out into the Firth to offset the shallow shoreline. There is a fine signal box beside the railway bridge, a small lighthouse and various monuments to Thomas Telford. Upstream of the Muirtown basin is the final flight of locks.

- Two miles west of the centre, the vitrified fort of Craig Phadrig dates from around 350 BC. Walk through mixed woodlands to its hilltop site for superb views overlooking Inverness and its hinterland (one hour round trip from the car park).

- Five miles to the east, on the B9006, is Culloden, where the Jacobites were finally defeated in 1746. A ceremony is held every year on the anniversary (16 April). The site is open year-round, and its visitor centre is open daily from February to December (telephone 01463 790 607). One mile to the east lies Clava Cairns (page 29), also open year-round.

- Eleven miles to the north east is Fort George, an outstanding Georgian artillery fort that still has a working garrison. It was built by William Skinner between 1745-69 to house up to 2000 troops. However, after Culloden its military purpose of suppressing the Jacobites was no longer relevant. It features reconstructions and displays of muskets and pikes, and is open daily all year (telephone 01667 462 777).

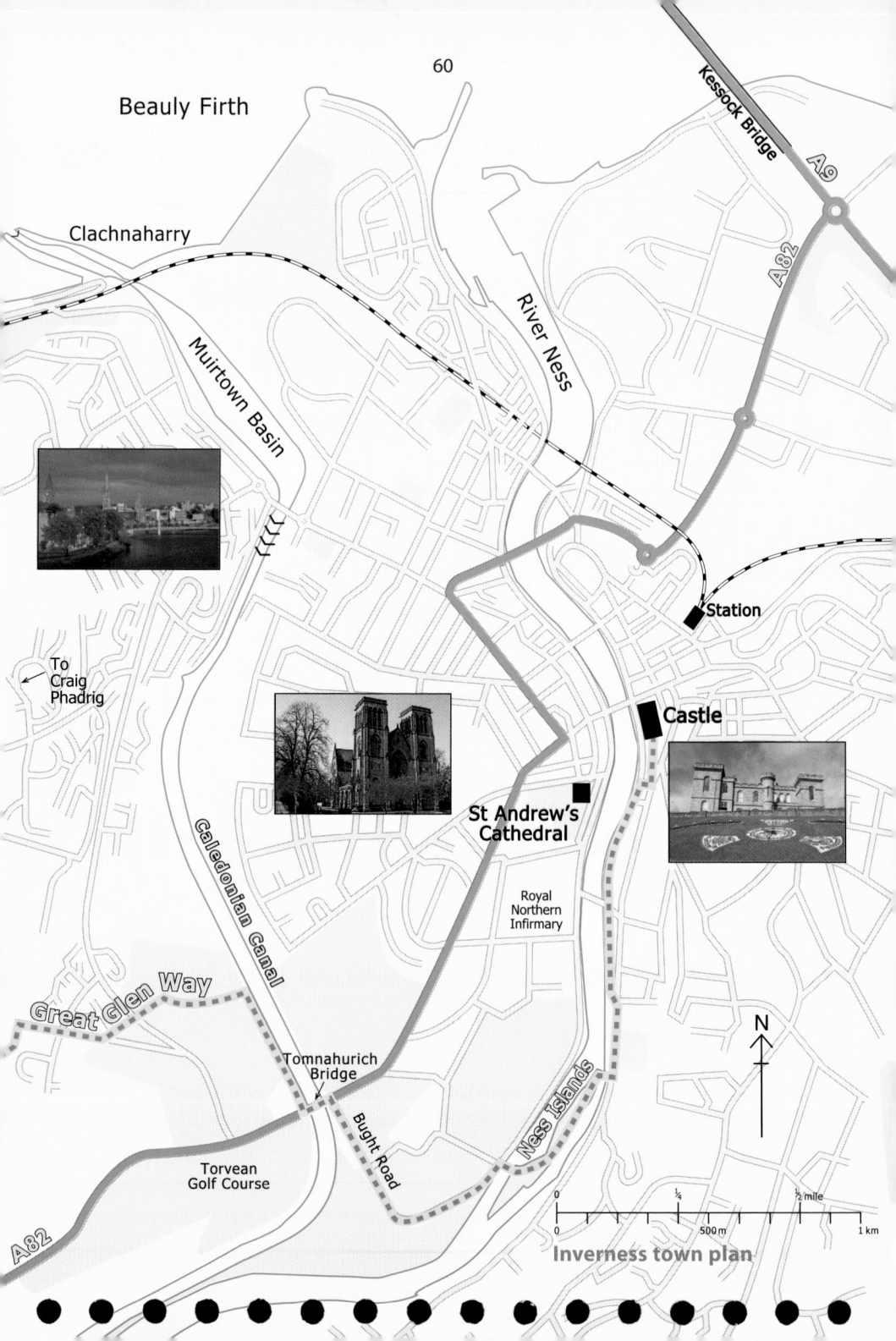

Beauly Firth

Kessock Bridge

A9

A82

Clachnaharry

River Ness

Muirtown Basin

To Craig Phadrig

Station

Castle

St Andrew's Cathedral

Caledonian Canal

Royal Northern Infirmary

Great Glen Way

Tomnahurich Bridge

Bught Road

Ness Islands

N

Torvean Golf Course

A82

0   ¼   ½ mile
0   500 m   1 km

Inverness town plan

Reference

Contact details

All telephone numbers are shown as dialled from within the UK. To dial from another country, use the access code then 44 followed by the number below minus its leading zero. Details were checked before publication, but phone numbers and website URLs are liable to change without notice.

To contact the Great Glen Way Route Manager, write to:

The Great Glen Way Office
Auchteraw
Fort Augustus
PH32 4BT
Phone/fax   01320 366 633
website   www.greatglenway.com

Forestry Commission

The Forestry Commission is responsible for managing, protecting and expanding Britain's forests and woodlands, with the aim of increasing their value to society and the environment. The FC's two Forest Districts are Fort Augustus (01320 366322) and Lochaber (01397 702184). It publishes various illustrated leaflets on the Great Glen Forest Walks and on the Great Glen Cycle Route. Request them free from its Inverness office:

Forest Enterprise Scotland (North)
1 Highlander Way
Inverness Business Park
Inverness
IV2 7GB
Phone   01463 232 811
Fax   01463 243 846

Tourist Information Centres

The umbrella organisation is the Highlands of Scotland Tourist Board (HOST):

Peffery House
Strathpeffer
Ross-shire
IV14 9HA
Phone   01997 421 160

HOST publishes many brochures on the highlands, incuding two local visitor guides (Fort William and Lochaber; and Inverness, Loch Ness and Nairn) with maps, visitor information and accommodation listings (free on request). Their website **www.host.co.uk** is well worth a visit.

Four TICs are on the Way, open year-round except from October to Easter when Fort Augustus is closed and Drumnadrochit has restricted hours:

Fort William   01397 703 781
Fort Augustus   01320 366 367
Drumnadrochit   [contact HOST]
Inverness   01463 234 353

Highland Council operates the Glen Nevis Visitor Centre: 01397 705 922

Service providers

The Scottish Activity Holiday Association maintains a register of providers, see their website at **www.activity-scotland.co.uk**. Here are some established operators who offer booking and support services:

C-N-Do   01786 445 703
                    info@cndoscotland.com

Easyways   01324 714 132
                    info@easyways.com

Make Tracks   0131 229 6844
                    mtracks@dircon.co.uk

Transcotland   01887 820 848
                    info@transcotland.com

Bespoke Highland Tours
                    0141 334 9017
                    bespoke.tours@virgin.net

Caledonian Canal and boat charter

Caledonian Canal Office
Seaport Marina
Muirtown Wharf
Inverness
IV3 5LS
Phone   01463 233 140

The canal operates from 0800 to 1730 on weekdays, and in summer is open also at weekends; sea locks are tidal. Check their website for latest information: www.scottishcanals.co.uk

For boat charter, contact:
Caley Cruisers Ltd
Canal Road
Inverness
IV3 8NF
Phone   01463 236 328
website   www.caleycruisers.com

Scottish Youth Hostel Association (SYHA)

The SYHA is a registered charity that operates youth hostels and provides a useful website with full details; it also accepts online bookings. Membership costs £6 pa (2001) or you can pay a non-member supplement of £1 per night; no upper age limit, sheet sleeping bag provided, prices range from £7-£14 per night.

7 Glebe Crescent
Stirling
FK8 2JA
Phone   01786 891 400
website   www.syha.org.uk

Transport

Scottish Citylink (buses)
    08705 505 050   www.citylink.co.uk

Railtrack (UK railways)
    08457 484 950   www.railtrack.co.uk

easyJet
    0870 6000 000   www.easyjet.com

Glasgow Airport   0141 887 1111

Edinburgh Airport   0131 333 1000

Inverness Airport   01463 232 471

Other websites

There are hundreds of sites relevant to the Great Glen, Loch Ness and the historical background. The Loch Ness 2000 Project maintains a superb resource on the scientific explorations: **www.loch-ness-scotland.com** – visit the archive room for its rich store of documents.

The Royal Commission on Ancient and Historic Monuments maintains a database on interesting sites, including the Great Glen hill forts:

www.rcahms.gov.uk/canmore.html

The Scottish Highland Photo Library (see photo credits) has a website at www.stockscotland.com (phone 01862 892 298, email shpl@cali.co.uk).

Scottish Natural Heritage has a website at www.snh.org.uk.

Further reading

All books recommended below are low-priced and lightweight. Where possible, ISBNs are given to assist readers from outside the UK.

Ben Nevis and Glen Nevis: Wildlife and Geology (1989) 22-page booklet from the then Nature Conservancy Council for Scotland, now Scottish Natural Heritage   ISBN 0 86139 589 1

Cameron, A D (1995) *Introducing the Caledonian Canal* 36-page booklet from Firtree Publishing Ltd   ISBN 1 872825 00 1

Inverness, Loch Ness and Nairn (30-page tourist board booklet, no date or ISBN))

The Great Glen: Wildlife and Landscape (1991) 26-page booklet from the then Nature Conservancy Council for Scotland, now Scottish Natural Heritage   ISBN 0 86139 691 X

Sinclair, Charles (1998) *A Wee Guide to the Jacobites* 88 pages,   ISBN 1 899874 14 3

Tabraham, C and Stewart, F *Urquhart Castle: the Official Souvenir Guide* Historic Scotland
    ISBN 0 7480 0601 X

Acknowledgements

The author is very grateful to the following people for support of various kinds, especially for detailed comments on the manuscript in draft: Tony Dyer and the Highland Council's Great Glen Way Steering Group, Alastair MacLeod, Sir Robert Megarry, Adrian Shine, Sandra Bardwell, Malcolm Wield, Sandra Paul, Keir Bloomer, Fraser Campbell (Drumnadrochit Hotel), Dave Hewitt, Julie Deans and Ian Pragnell. Their efforts resulted in many improvements, but we accept responsibility for any flaws. We welcome comments from readers, preferably by email to info@rucsacs.com.

Rucksack Readers

Rucksack Readers cover three of the four Long Distance Routes in Scotland (see page 4). Two others are uniform with this volume:

The Speyside Way by J Megarry and J Strachan (Buckie to Aviemore, up to 84 miles) 2000

The West Highland Way by J Megarry (Glasgow to Fort William, 95 miles) 2000

Selected international walks are also available in very similar format, eg:

Explore Mount Kilimanjaro by J Megarry (Tanzania, altitude 19,340 feet/5896 m) 2001.

For more information, or to order online, visit **www.rucsacs.com**. To order by telephone, dial 01786 824 696 (+44 1786 824 696 outside UK).

Maps

The Ordnance Survey Landranger Series scale is 1:50,000 (sheets 26, 34 and 41). For side-trips, more detailed maps are essential: the OS Pathfinder/Explorer scale is 1:25,000. Harvey's Map Services publishes a Superwalker (1:25,000) for Ben Nevis, and is due to publish a complete route map for the Way (www.harveymaps.co.uk).

Photo credits

The publisher is grateful to the following for permission to reproduce their images: Argyll, the Isles, Loch Lomond, Stirling and Trossachs Tourist Board (p37), Caley Cruisers (p25), Clan Cameron Museum (p43), Forestry Commission (p34 upper, p35 lower two, p36 upper), Highlands of Scotland Tourist Board (p17, p20, p41 lower, p44, p47, p48, p50, p52 lower, p54, p57, p59, back cover), Loch Ness 2000 (p22, p53), Angus and Patricia Macdonald (front cover), NERC Satellite Receiving Station, University of Dundee (p23), Royal Society for the Protection of Birds (p33 lower), Scottish Highland Photo Library (p9, p32 upper and lower, p34 lower, p35 upper, p36 lower right, p37 upper, p38, p39, p40, p58 upper), Colin Simpson (p1, p27 upper, p29 lower, p30, p42, p46 lower, p51, p56, p58 lower, p60 all three); 17 other images ©Jacquetta Megarry.

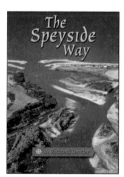

ISBN 1-898481-08-3

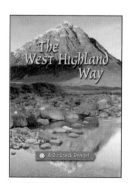

ISBN 1-898481-09-1

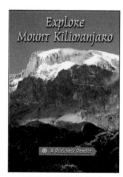

ISBN 1-898481-10-5

info@rucsacs.com   www.rucsacs.com